The Brooklyn Bridge, 1883

Cornerstones of Freedom

The Story of
THE
BROOKLYN
BRIDGE

By Zachary Kent

CHILDRENS PRESS ®
CHICAGO

Currier and Ives 1877 etch of the Brooklyn Bridge

Library of Congress Cataloging-in-Publication Data

Kent, Zachary.
   The story of the Brooklyn Bridge / by Zachary Kent.
      p.   cm. — (Cornerstones of freedom)
   Includes index.
   Summary: Chronicles the design and construction of the
nineteenth-century suspension bridge linking Brooklyn and
Manhattan which took fourteen years to complete and claimed
several lives.
   ISBN 0-516-04739-6
   1.   Brooklyn Bridge (New York, N.Y.) — History — Juvenile
literature. 2.   New York (N.Y.) — Buildings, structures, etc. — Juvenile
literature. [1. Brooklyn Bridge (New York, N.Y.) 2.   Bridge
construction.] I. Title. II. Series.
TG25.N53K46   1988   88-16220
624'.55'097471 — dc19   CIP
                                             AC

Childrens Press®, Chicago

On May 24, 1883 thousands of people jammed the streets of New York and Brooklyn. On both sides of the East River joyful crowds packed waterfront wharves, filled rooftops, and leaned from windows to witness the dedication of the Brooklyn Bridge.

Nothing compared to this new suspension bridge, the longest in the world. Its roadway stretched more than a mile; its twin towers jutted higher into the sky than the tallest buildings in sight. Proud Brooklynites and New Yorkers recalled how hundreds of workmen labored fourteen years to finish the impressive bridge. They gazed in wonder at the steel suspension cables hanging in a well-ordered pattern like harp strings, holding the bridge firmly in place.

Sidewalk vendors hawked pictures of the bridge, bridge buttons, ribbons, and memorial medals. Brass bands blared, and flags snapped in the springtime breeze. On the river, boats of many sizes formed a grand and colorful flotilla. Outside the Fifth Avenue Hotel in Manhattan, New Yorkers yelled happy greetings as U.S. President Chester A. Arthur climbed into an open carriage. With a mounted police escort and marching soldiers, President Arthur rode down Broadway and onto the bridge roadway. At the New York tower, he stepped from his carriage to walk the final distance across.

THE SIGNAL TO FIRE THE PRESIDENTIAL SALUTE

MAYOR LOW RECEIVING THE PRESIDENT

COMIC BALLOONS

Opening
of the
Brooklyn
Bridge,
1883

While President Arthur made his triumphant march, cannons were fired at nearby Fort Hamilton, at the Brooklyn Navy Yard, and on the five U.S. warships stationed on the river. Factory whistles joined the screaming chorus of tugboat, steamboat, and ferry whistles. Church bells clanged, and along the riverfront thousands of people cheered. The New York *Sun* reported, "the climax of fourteen years' suspense seemed to have been reached [as] the President of the United States of America... walked dry shod to Brooklyn from New York."

One deserving man, however, was unable to take part in the grand celebration. In his house on Brooklyn's distant Columbia Heights, forty-six-year-old Washington Roebling sat in his upstairs bedroom.

Washington Roebling oversaw the construction of the bridge from his home.

With a pair of binoculars he gazed at the excitement from his window. His father, John A. Roebling, had designed the magnificent bridge, and as its chief engineer, Washington Roebling had sacrificed years of his life to carry out its construction. The work had left him badly crippled. Now, noises pained his sensitive hearing and long conversations left him exhausted.

Everyone recognized that this day of thrilling accomplishment really served as a day of tribute to the Roeblings. "With one name, this Bridge will always be associated—that of *Roebling*," bridge trustee William C. Kingsley warmly remarked at the dedication ceremony. Without the vision and guiding spirits of the father and son, the Brooklyn Bridge surely never could have been built.

For two hundred years farming and trading settlements had thrived on New York's Manhattan Island and on Long Island just across the East River. As the cities of New York and Brooklyn rapidly grew, ferryboats carried travelers back and forth across the river. Days of fog, rain, and storm, however, often caused delays, and when winter ice clogged the river, ferry passengers sometimes shivered for hours waiting for a chance to cross. By the 1800s citizens wanted a better method of transportation. "New York and Brooklyn must be

Brooklyn ferry in 1750, crossing from Brooklyn to Manhattan Island

united," declared New York *Tribune* editor Horace Greeley in 1849.

At last in April 1867 the state government granted a charter to the New York Bridge Company "for the purpose of constructing and maintaining a bridge over the East River . . ." To build the bridge the company trustees chose sixty-year-old John A. Roebling. A Trenton, New Jersey, wire manufacturer and brilliant engineer, Roebling already had built several important river bridges. Promptly he submitted plans for the East River project. "The completed work," he announced, "when constructed in accordance with my designs, will not only be the

John A. Roebling (right)
designed the Brooklyn Bridge.
It had a promenade,
carriage roadway, and railroad.

greatest bridge in existence, but it will be the greatest engineering work of the continent, and of the age." The bridge that Roebling proposed would be the longest in the world with a carriage roadway as well as a railroad for commuters. He also promised to include a walkway for pedestrians. "This elevated promenade," he declared, "will allow people of leisure . . . to stroll over the bridge on fine days, in order to enjoy the beautiful views and pure air."

As soon as his plans were approved, Roebling embarked upon the greatest effort of his famous life. On June 28, 1869, the engineer began surveying the bridge route at the Brooklyn Fulton Ferry slip. While yelling instructions to his survey team, he failed to notice a ferryboat steaming into dock. When the boat entered the slip it caught and crushed the end of Roebling's right boot between the wooden piling. Workers carried the injured chief engineer to his son's Brooklyn home and a doctor soon amputated his mangled toes. Everyone hoped for Roebling's speedy recovery. Sadly, however, tetanus (lockjaw) developed, and after suffering days of rigid agony, John A. Roebling died on July 22, 1869. Superstitious people whispered that the start of every bridge claimed at least one life. The loss of Roebling, though, seemed an especially shocking twist of fate.

Washington A. Roebling in 1870

The bridge trustees worried whether the project could even continue. Quickly they offered the position of chief engineer to Roebling's thirty-two-year-old son, Washington. No living man better understood the bridge's design. As his father's closest assistant, Colonel Washington Roebling had been building bridges for eleven years. While a Union officer during the American Civil War he had constructed two important military bridges.

Washington Roebling eagerly took up his father's work. He immediately assembled an engineering staff, ordered derricks, drills, and assorted supplies. First, the bridge towers must be built on solid foundations. At the site of the Brooklyn tower on January 2, 1870, laborers began tearing out an existing pier and scooping mud from the riverbed with dredging machinery.

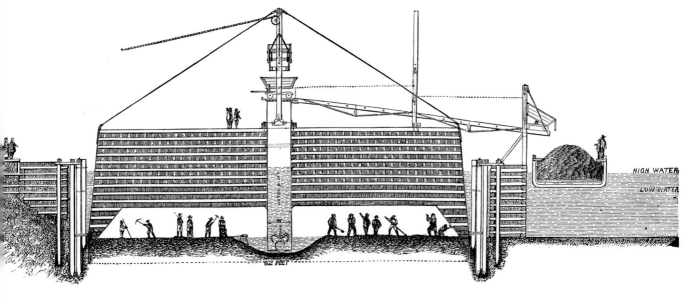

Cross-section of the Brooklyn caisson

To dig even deeper to reach rock bottom, Roebling ordered the construction of a huge "caisson" at a shipyard four miles up the river. Half the size of a city block, the box-shaped caisson measured 168 feet long and 102 feet wide. Fifteen tightly seamed layers of pine timbers provided a strong roof. Inside the caisson there was nine and a half feet of headroom. Also, support walls divided the open area into six separate chambers. Completely sheathed with tin, caulking, and thick iron boiler plate, the caisson would be airtight. Inside this structure, Roebling expected workmen to dig away at the riverbed, while at the same time stonemasons built the 277-foot Brooklyn tower upon its roof.

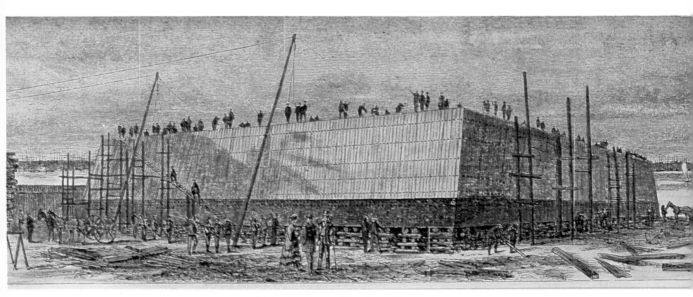

Exterior view of the Brooklyn caisson

On March 19, 1870, hundreds of spectators watched in wonder as six tugboats towed the 3,000-ton-Brooklyn caisson down the East River. Then Roebling's assistant engineers carefully sank the giant structure exactly at the spot for the Brooklyn tower. When only the roof showed above the river's surface, powerful air pumps next pushed the water out of the box and kept it out.

Roebling paid his Irish, German, and Italian immigrant workers $2.25 a day. By June 1870 these laborers were hard at work. On the roof of the caisson men used hoists and steam engines to guide blocks of granite and limestone into place. Inside the strange, cavelike caisson, teams of diggers called "sandhogs" swung picks and shoveled dirt.

During each shift the men entered the caisson's compressed air chambers through two air-lock shafts in the roof. The temperature inside remained a constant hot and humid eighty degrees. The compressed air within the chambers also affected the men. Master mechanic E. F. Farrington recalled, "Inside the caisson everything wore an unreal, weird appearance. There was a confused sensation in the head, like 'the rush of many waters.' The pulse at first was accelerated, and then sometimes fell below the normal rate. The voice sounded faint and unnatural, and it became a great effort to speak. What with the flaming light, the deep shadows, the confusing noise of hammers, drills, and chains . . . time passed quickly in the caisson."

Sandhogs worked inside the caisson.

Also built into the caisson roof were two additional shafts that contained dredge buckets, which opened and closed like clamshells. Men with wheelbarrows carried loads of sand, mud, and broken rock to the bases of these shafts. Then the dredge buckets were used to haul the material out. When picks and hammers failed to break large boulders, the workers carefully used explosives.

"The work of the buried bridgebuilder," exclaimed the New York *Herald*, "... does not cease for the sun at noonday or the silent stars at night. Gangs are relieved and replaced and perspiring companies of men follow each other up and down the iron locks with a dim quiet purpose..." During eight-hour shifts the sandhogs (a total work force of about 264 men) cut away the riverbed beneath them. The caisson sank at a rate of six to eighteen inches a week. Sometimes air suddenly escaped from the caisson and shot up to the river surface spewing water and mud on nearby wharves, passing boats, and frightened bystanders. The worst "blowout" occurred on a Sunday when no one was at work. With a deafening roar all of the caisson's compressed air escaped up one of the dredging shafts. A geyser of mud and stone shot five hundred feet into the air. Stunned by the thunderous sound, people rushed to the river. "Even the toll-collectors at the

View of Brooklyn caisson after the 1870 fire

ferry abandoned their tills," commented Roebling.

On December 2, 1870, the success of the caisson was threatened when workmen discovered a raging fire hidden in the timbers above their heads. Roebling guessed that a laborer had sparked the blaze by accidentally holding a candle too close to a caulked roof seam. Quickly the spark burned deep into the layered timbers. Men sprayed water and fire extinguishers into the open hole, but some red hot coals still burned. Fearing that further burning would cause the weakened caisson roof to collapse, Roebling ordered the air chambers flooded. Three fireboats and engines from the Brooklyn fire department pumped in over a million gallons of water. Filling every crack and crevice, the flood soaked the last of the fire's glowing embers.

Although the fire slowed progress, the Brooklyn caisson finally reached bedrock at a depth of forty-five feet. Workmen filled the air chambers with concrete, and upon this solid foundation stonemasons continued to build the Brooklyn tower. Soon afterwards across the river a second caisson was sunk on September 11, 1871. Work inside the New York caisson progressed much more speedily. Few boulders hampered the diggers and its two clamshell dredges easily scooped up loads of sand. In addition Roebling designed some fifty-eight sand pipes, extending from the chamber floors up through the caisson roof. Men shoveled sand, dirt, and fine gravel near the mouths of these pipes where the chambers' high air pressure forced the material up and out. The sand blasted from the pipes with such power that one day a boatman rowing past the site had the end of a finger shot off by a ricocheting pebble.

Although digging proved easier, the New York caisson had to sink much deeper before reaching bedrock. Therefore, with each passing day the laborers suffered more from the effects of the compressed air. For every two feet that the caisson sank, the pressure inside increased another pound. As a result, the men sometimes experienced fatigue, dizziness, and other symptoms of the dreaded "caisson disease" also known as the bends. Doctors in the 1870s did not understand that people leaving an atmosphere of compressed air need rest-time for "decompression" to act upon their bodies. Otherwise, the rapid release of the nitrogen bubbles built up in their blood may cause great harm. As the New York caisson sank below fifty and sixty feet, the caisson disease struck more often.

After leaving the air chambers at the end of their work shifts, some men broke out in cold sweats and experienced blurred vision, numbness, and faintness. Others doubled over with severe leg and stomach cramps. It felt "as if the flesh were being torn from the bones," moaned one victim. Between January and June of 1872 the bridge company doctor treated 110 cases of caisson disease.

Engineers and workers atop the Brooklyn tower September, 1872

When the New York caisson reached seventy-one feet, the first death occurred. Feeling ill after his workday, John Myers dropped dead while climbing the stairs of his boardinghouse. Within a month, two other laborers also died of the disease. At a depth of seventy-eight and a half feet the New York caisson rested on soil so tightly compacted together that it was hard as rock. Roebling believed it would support the New York tower. Rather than risk more lives, he ordered the digging stopped on May 18, 1872.

Roebling himself had spent many hours inside the caissons. Now, while directing the pouring of concrete inside the New York caisson in the spring of 1872, he suffered a severe attack of the bends. For several days in awful pain, the chief engineer lingered on the brink of death. Although he slowly improved, his arms and legs often ached. He tired easily and often felt nauseous. His eyesight dimmed and most noises hurt his ears. He remained, however, dedicated to his work. Through the next painful months, he carefully wrote out page after page of instructions, drawings, and diagrams for his assistant engineers to follow in case he should die.

A long visit to a German spa failed to restore Roebling's health. In 1873, he returned to the Roebling family home in Trenton, New Jersey, and rested there for three more years. During that time his faithful assistants kept work on the bridge moving ahead. Bridge stonemasons set the last granite block atop the Brooklyn tower in June 1875. In July of the following year the New York tower finally stood as high as its twin across the river. During this time wagons hauled away the rubble of houses torn down to make way for the bridge's roadway approaches. Two great anchorages were built to hold the bridge's cable ends securely in place. With pulleys and winches workmen heaved the massive cable-making machinery into position. The bridge was halfway finished.

In 1876 Roebling returned to Brooklyn. From the upstairs window of his Columbia Heights house, he watched the workers. His body still wrecked, and under nervous strain, he remained unable to visit the work site personally or even talk to his assistants. Instead, his loving wife Emily carefully and expertly delivered his instructions.

Emily Warren Roebling, 1880

By this time citizens daily gathered along the East River to watch the stringing of the bridge cables. On August 14, 1876, a tugboat pulled the first wire rope through the water across the river. Made of twisted steel wires, the 3,400-foot rope was hauled to the top of the New York tower. Later a second rope followed and their ends were spliced together. Curving around great drums from anchorage to anchorage, the rope could now be drawn back and forth like a huge clothesline. "Wedded," exclaimed the Brooklyn *Eagle* when the ends were joined. Hanging high above the river, this "traveler" rope connected the two towers for the first time.

To give his cable-riggers courage to do the dangerous work that lay before them, master mechanic E. F. Farrington decided to take the first ride across the river on August 25, 1876. As an engine turned the traveler drums, the rope drew Farrington, sitting on a narrow wooden slat, up from the Brooklyn anchorage to the top of the Brooklyn tower. After walking across the tower roof, Farrington sat on the wooden slat again. The traveler then towed him across the East River. To the hundreds of thousands of thrilled witnesses Farrington seemed like an insect dangling on a thread. The mass of boats on the river let their whistles loudly shriek, and in answer to the yelling crowds Farrington happily waved. In

Farrington crossed the East River while 10,000 New Yorkers watched

just twenty-two minutes the spry fifty-nine-year-old workman traveled from anchorage to anchorage. "The ride gave me a magnificent view," he later declared, "and such pleasing sensations as probably I shall never experience again . . ."

Catwalk across the East River

In the following days Roebling's engineers super-
vised the stringing of a second traveler, a narrow
catwalk, and additional wire ropes to support "cra-
dles," which were long wooden platforms that the
cable-riggers could stand on while binding the wires
for the great cables. Each day curious crowds
watched the fearless riggers swaying high in the
breeze. The New York *Tribune* reported: "With its
princes of the lofty wire, the Brooklyn Bridge is now
the cheapest, the most entertaining, and the best-
attended circus in the world."

Many people found the catwalk of special interest.
Its wooden slats measured just four feet wide and it
possessed only simple wire rope railings. Soon after
this temporary footbridge opened in February 1877,

C. C. Martin, a bridge engineer, invited his children to walk it with him. The sight of Martin's two daughters stepping out between the bridge tower completely surprised passengers on the Fulton Ferry far below. "Beauty on the Bridge" exclaimed a story the next day in the New York *Illustrated Times*. As many as three thousand visitors later obtained passes to walk the narrow catwalk.

With the guide wires in place, the job of cable making began. In the Brooklyn workyard laborers dipped great coils of steel wire in tubs of molten zinc. This "galvanizing" process strengthened the wire and protected it from the salt air. Next two metal "carrier" wheels (like bicycle wheels held upright between two wire ropes) towed the galvanized

Cable
wrapping
1878

Each cable (left) was made of hundreds of wires. On June 14, 1878 a cable snapped and wildly hurled wires across the bridge. Two men died and several were injured.

wire back and forth from anchorage to anchorage. When three hundred wires were pulled across, cable-riggers twisted and compressed them into a single strand 3/4″ in diameter. When nineteen strands were finished, the riggers clamped and wrapped them together to make one of the bridge's four giant cables.

Day in and day out the wire stringing progressed. "The network of wires across the East River is rapidly beginning to look something like a bridge," commented the New York *Herald* in August 1877. Bad weather sometimes halted the work. Lack of money and a political scandal involving bridge stockholders also slowed Roebling's schedule. But with each passing season, the sickly engineer remained at his window and watched the bridge gradually take shape.

As the years passed the bridge claimed more lives. A dozen men died during the building of the towers and the roadways leading to them. One worker died when he rolled his wheelbarrow off the edge of a narrow plank. In panic he clung tightly to the handles instead of letting go.

On June 14, 1878, another tragedy occurred. A cable strand suddenly snapped, hurling wires across the New York anchorage. One man died instantly and another died when knocked eighty feet to the ground. Whipping wire ends cut a nearby telephone pole in half and clipped a chimney off a house.

It remained a mystery why that particular strand broke. Later, though, Roebling discovered that a crooked contractor was supplying the bridge company with faulty wire. Of this wire fraud he exclaimed, "An engineer who has not been educated as a spy or detective is no match for a rascal." Luckily, Roebling had designed the cables to be six times stronger than necessary. For extra safety he now ordered 150 additional wires woven into each of the four cables.

The cable making process required years of careful work. Some impatient bridge trustees blamed the slowness on Roebling's poor health. They felt that if Roebling's mind was failing he ought to be replaced as chief engineer. Trustee John T. Agnew, however, quickly defended the sickly bridgebuilder. He said that Roebling could easily watch the progress from his room with his field glasses. "His plans and diagrams are all about him, and nothing is done in the work until it has first been submitted to him." By a vote of ten to seven the trustees decided that Roebling was too important to lose.

In the summer of 1878 the Brooklyn *Eagle* reported, "The thousands who daily cross the ferries and look up to the lofty towers . . . note the strands that stretch across the intervening space, [and] hardly realize that the cable making of the structure is nearing its completion." After the riggers clamped and wrapped the last cable, they next attached the wire rope suspenders. Loops in the suspenders would hold the steel floor beams of the bridge roadway. All through 1880 the steel bridge

Engineers survey the progress of the suspension bridge in 1881.

On the promenade of the Brooklyn Bridge 1895

floor slowly advanced across the river. After riveting the sections together, workmen next lay the wooden planks of the roadway. Building the railroad tracks and terminal buildings took time, as did painting the bridge and hammering down the wooden promenade deck.

At last in the spring of 1883 the bridge trustees excitedly announced the finish of the "New York and Brooklyn Bridge." They sent out thirteen thousand special invitations to the opening day ceremonies scheduled for May 24. On that gala day hundreds of thousands of visitors crowded near the bridge's tall granite towers and stood along its arching roadway. As cannons roared, and people cheered, President Chester A. Arthur led the first official walk across. During the speeches that followed, Brooklyn mayor Seth Low declared, "The beautiful and stately structure fulfills the fondest hope. . . . The impression upon the visitor is one of astonishment that grows with every visit."

The opening of the Brooklyn Bridge was a national event. After fourteen years of labor, Americans freely bragged that it was the "Eighth Wonder of the World." To congratulate its chief engineer, President Arthur paid a special visit to Roebling's house and shook his hand. The crippled engineer had succeeded in spite of long delays and hardship. That night as a colorful fireworks display filled the sky above the bridge, surely Roebling felt the pride that rightfully belonged to him.

Today the Brooklyn Bridge remains an emblem of engineering genius and personal sacrifice. Through the years millions of people have paid their tolls and driven wagons and carriages, and later automobiles and trucks, over its wide roadway. Thousands of passengers have ridden the commuter trains along its rattling railroad tracks, and untold numbers have strolled and jogged upon its promenade for exercise and pleasure. "Nothing lasts forever," Washington Roebling once warned, but after more than a century the celebrated Brooklyn Bridge endures.

View of Brooklyn Bridge, 1895

About the Author

    Zachary Kent grew up in the town of Little Falls, New Jersey. He is a graduate of St. Lawrence University and holds a teaching certificate in English. Following college he was employed at a New York City literary agency for two years until he decided to launch a career as a writer. To support himself while writing, he has worked as a taxi driver, a shipping clerk, and a house painter.

    Mr. Kent has had a lifelong interest in American history. As a boy the study of the United States presidents was his special hobby. His collection of presidential items includes books, pictures, and games, as well as several autographed letters.